P9-CMY-765

Growing Up Wild

PENGUINS

Other Books by Sandra Markle

Also

Growing Up Wild
PENGUINS

Sandra Markle

Atheneum Books for Young Readers
New York London Toronto Sydney Singapore

Central Islip Public Library
33 Hawthorne Avenue
Central Islip, NY 11722-2498

191 1664

Antarctica

Adelie penguins live in one of the coldest places on Earth, Antarctica. They spend most of the year in the Antarctic seas living on the *pack ice,* resting on floating ice rafts and diving under the ice to catch food. Then in September and October, they head for the coast of Antarctica. That's springtime in the southern hemisphere, and thousands of Adelie penguins gather in *colonies* to mate and raise their young at places like Cape Royds and Cape Bird on Ross Island.

Adelie penguins begin to nest once they are about three to four years old. The males are the first to reach the colony. Each male stakes out a nest site and builds a nest platform by carrying pebbles to the site one stone at a time.

When the females arrive, each male stands at his nest, points his beak skyward, and trumpets. Penguins often choose the same mate year after year. Within a few days of mating, the female lays an egg. About four to five days later, she lays a second, slightly smaller egg.

Now comes the task of incubating the eggs, keeping them warm and dry. To do this job, penguins have a special pocket of bare skin called a *brood pouch*. Usually the breast muscles press the two sides of the pouch together, sealing it shut. During the *incubation* period, though, the parent relaxes these muscles to open the pouch. Warm blood flowing through the bare skin in the pouch warms the eggs. From time to time, the parent turns the eggs with its feet to keep them evenly warm. It can take thirty-three to thirty-nine days for the chick to develop.

Because the parent incubating the eggs can't go to sea to feed, the pair takes turns caring for the eggs. Laying eggs uses up energy, so the female usually goes to sea first. Then the parents switch off about every twelve to fifteen days.

A platform of stones may seem like a silly nest, but it's just right for Adelie penguins. A stone nest drains well if it snows and the snow melts. Wet eggs are likely to chill the growing chick inside. This can slow the chick's development, maybe even kill it.

A penguin's nest is always under construction. The parent returning from a feeding trip takes time to bring a few new pebbles to the parent on duty. Sometimes the gift stones are snatched from a neighbor's nest. In this way stones slowly migrate from nest to nest in the colony.

Adelie parents must also guard their young from gull-like birds called *skuas*. The skuas nest on the edges of the penguin colony. They feed on penguin eggs and later on penguin chicks.

While Adelie parents are always on the alert for skuas, the way they respond to an attack puts their babies at risk. When a skua swoops down, the parents stand up, squawking at the intruder to scare it away. But skuas often hunt in mated pairs. So while the first skua distracts the parents, the second snatches an egg or a chick.

Finally, a chick is ready to hatch. It uses a special bump on its beak, called an *egg tooth*, to peck a hole in the shell. This is hard work for the chick, especially working from inside the egg. It may take a chick two to three days to break out.

Because the two eggs were laid several days apart, one chick hatches before the other, giving it a head start eating and growing.

A newly hatched chick is so weak that just turning its head is likely to send it sprawling. The chick's flippers have not yet hardened, so when it flaps, its rubbery flippers flop and wiggle. The Adelie parents tuck their young chicks into their brood pouch to keep them warm and safe.

Because of the weather and the skuas, penguin parents have to work hard to have even one of their two chicks survive to grow up.

A growing chick's whole life is focused on eating. When it's hungry, the chick pokes its head out of the brood pouch, peeping loudly. The parent bends its neck down, opens its mouth, and squeezes its stomach muscles to bring up some food. The chick pokes its beak into its parent's mouth and gobbles up its meal. Eating often, the chick quickly grows bigger and stronger. It also loses its egg tooth after the first few days.

While a newly hatched chick needs its parent's brood pouch to stay warm, the youngster quickly grows a woolly coat of long, soft *down* so it can stay warm on its own. That's lucky, because the chick is soon so big that all it can squeeze into its parent's brood pouch is its head!

During the first couple of weeks after the chick hatches, the parents take turns guarding it and going to sea for food. When the feeding parent returns, the adults go through a special greeting, bending their heads together toward their chicks, waving their necks and calling. This joyous display, which is repeated several times, seems to say, "Wow! I'm okay. You're okay. Our chicks are okay." Then the parents switch duties.

Central Islip Public Library
33 Hawthorne Avenue
Central Islip, NY 11722-2498

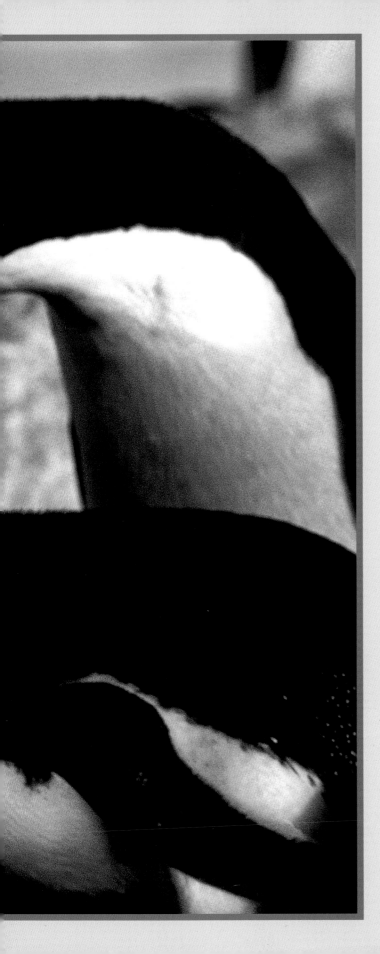

The parent who remains on the nest to guard the chicks is very protective. It is likely to snap angrily at another penguin, as well as at a skua that comes too close to its nest. Sometimes, the parent will even leap off its nest to drive away the intruder, squawking and flapping its flippers. Because the adult Adelie flippers are hard and the muscles that move them are strong, flipper whacks can feel like being smacked with a wooden paddle, and the smacks may be repeated many times in a minute.

The parent whose turn it is to bring back food for the chicks must first
travel across the pack ice to open water. That may be a distance of a few feet
or many miles. The penguin may walk or it may toboggan, flopping down on
its belly and using its flippers like oars to row across the ice.

To collect food, the Adelie parent dives under the ice in search of shrimplike krill and small silvery fish that collect there. Spines on the penguin's tongue help it hang on to its slippery meal. The penguin holds its breath while it dives, so it must repeatedly return to the surface for air.

Penguins must watch out for *orcas,* or killer whales, since orcas like to eat penguins. So do *leopard seals.* If the parent that has gone to sea to find food is delayed too long or doesn't return, the parent on the nest will finally get too hungry to wait any longer. Then, it abandons its chick to go to sea to feed. When this happens, the chick usually dies.

A penguin chick alone would be quickly snatched up by hunting skuas who have babies of their own to feed.

By the time the chicks are about fifteen days old, both parents must begin going to sea to bring home food for their huge, hungry offspring. The chicks huddle together in groups called *créches* to stay safe and warm while their parents are away.

Skuas have a hard time grabbing a chick from a tightly packed créche. Nearby non-nesting adults are also likely to attack any skua that comes too close. They do this as a natural reaction to skuas rather than out of an instinct to protect the chicks.

When a parent returns with food, it goes to its nest site and calls out to the chick. Recognizing the sound, its chick comes running. Then the parent is likely to run off a short ways, wait until the chick nearly catches up, and then run on. This chase may help the chick exercise and grow stronger.

By the time they are about fifty days old, the chicks are nearly as big as their parents and their stomachs bulge with a two- to three-week food supply. Now the parents leave them forever, going out to catch food just for them-selves so they can get ready to *molt,* a process where they shed old feathers and grow new ones.

While living on their reserved food, the chicks shed their down and grow adult feathers. Finally, hunger draws the young adults to the ice edge.

Although they've never been in the water before, the young Adelies jump into the sea and begin to swim. They just naturally know how to swim the same way they know where to find food and how to catch it. For the next few years, the young Adelies will live on the pack ice while they mature. Then, one Antarctic spring, they'll head back to land to join the colony where they hatched. There they will build a nest, find a mate, and raise chicks of their own.

Glossary/Index

NOTE: Glossary words are italicized the first time they appear in the text.

BROOD POUCH (brüd 'pauch) Pouch of bare skin on the breast of both male and female Adelie penguins. This area has lots of blood vessels to radiate heat—just right for incubating eggs and warming newly hatched chicks. Muscles pull on both sides, sealing this pouch shut when it's not in use. 7, 15, 16, 19

COLONY (käl'ə nē) A group of penguins that gathers to mate and raise young. 5, 6, 8, 11, 30

CRÉCHE (kresh) A cluster of chicks huddled together for warmth and for safety in numbers while their parents are away hunting food. 28

DOWN (daun) Fluffy feathers that lack the tiny hooks that hold normal feather sections locked together. 19, 30

EGG TOOTH (eg 'tüth) Hard toothlike bump on the chick's beak that it uses to peck its way out of the shell. 13, 16

INCUBATION (in 'kyə bā 'shən) This is the process of keeping an egg warm and dry until the young inside has fully developed and pecked its way out of the egg. 7

LEOPARD SEAL (lep 'ərd sēl) As much as 3 meters (10 feet) long and weighing 272 kilograms (600 pounds), this spotted gray-and-black seal hunts alone on the pack ice. 25

MOLT (mōlt) The process of shedding old feathers and replacing them with new ones. 29

ORCA (ôrk ə) Powerful, toothed whales, also called killer whales, with black backs and white bellies. Males may grow to be about 9 meters (29 feet) long. Orcas travel and hunt in groups called pods. 25

PACK ICE (pak īs) Ice that builds up on water. Pack ice may be thin or thick. It is very important to Adelie penguins because the krill and fish they eat tend to stay just underneath the ice. 5, 24, 30

SKUAS (skyōō 'əs) Like the eagles of the Antarctic, these birds have sharp, curved talons and a hooked beak. Swooping in long arcs, skuas defend their hunting territory and their young. 11, 15, 23, 27, 28

ä as in c<u>a</u>rt   ā as in <u>a</u>pe   â as in <u>ai</u>r   ə as in b<u>a</u>nan<u>a</u>   ē as in <u>e</u>ven

ī as in b<u>i</u>te   ō as in g<u>o</u>   ü as in r<u>u</u>le   ʉ as in f<u>ur</u>

With love, for my husband, Yale Jeffery

Author's Note: There are many different kinds of penguins, such as yellow-eyed penguins that raise their young in New Zealand and Emperor penguins that hatch their chicks on the ice during the Antarctic winter. This book, though, is about just one kind of penguin—Adelies—and how they raise their chicks in large colonies.
The author would like to thank Dr. David Ainley (H.T. Harvey and Associates, San Jose, California) for sharing his expertise and enthusiasm.
Also a special thanks to Dr. Ainley's assistants Sacha Heath, Grant Ballard, Connie Adams, and Sophie Webb.

Photo Credits: Map courtesy of the National Science Foundation; all photos by Sandra Markle.

Atheneum Books for Young Readers
An imprint of Simon & Schuster Children's Publishing Division
1230 Avenue of the Americas
New York, New York 10020

Copyright © 2002 by Sandra Markle

All rights reserved, including the right of reproduction in whole
or in part in any form.

The text of this book is set in Berliner Grotesk.

Printed in Hong Kong

2 4 6 8 10 9 7 5 3 1

Library of Congress Cataloging-in-Publication Data
Markle, Sandra.
Growing up wild: penguins/ Sandra Markle. — 1st ed.
p. cm.
Summary: Depicts the hatching, care, growth, and education
of baby Adelie penguins.
ISBN 0-689-81887-4
1. Adelie penguins—Juvenile literature. [1 Adelie penguins.
2. Penguins. 3. Animals—Infancy.] I. Title.
QL696.S473M358   2002
598.47—dc21   99-023393

FIRST
EDITION